North of Crivitz

North of Crivitz

Poems by

Richard Holinger

Cover design by Shay Culligan

Cover and author photographs by Jay Holinger
(design@innstudiollc.com)
You capture the lake's mysticism and make me look authorly

ISBN: 978-1-952326-38-7

Kelsay Books
502 South 1040 East, A-119
American Fork, Utah, 84003

This book is for Tia, without whom the birds, the fish, the deer, the creek, the forest, the prairie, and the roads I've traveled are just that: birds, fish, deer, creek, forest, prairie, and roads. With you, they dance and sing, even the roads. Especially the roads.

In Appreciation

Because these poems have been written not only over the past years, but decades, there are many people to thank.

My former and present students at Marmion Academy on whom I tried many of these poems out, and who finger-snapped their approval.

The Elgin Community College Writers Center; the St. Charles Writers Group; and the Night Writers Workshop of Geneva, the latter two sponsored by their respective libraries. Thank you, workshop members, for your hours hunched over these lines and improving them.

Friends who read and encouraged these poems: Elburn poet Dave Etter, now gone; writer Pat Parks; colleague Alexander George.

For shaping and convincing the writer in me: Marvelwood School teacher Ed Sundt; Washington University poet Donald Finkel; University of Illinois at Chicago professor and poet Michael Anania; my brother, Bill Holinger.

Anne Veague and Kevin Moriarity for helping me and other writers promote our work at Waterline Writers of Batavia's Water Street Studios.

Karen Kelsay, this book's publisher, who believed in the poetry and kept me on task.

My family—Tia, Jay, and Molly—whose love and good cheer truly gave me the wellbeing that made these poems possible.

Finally, my grandfather, Lauren J. Drake, who bought a wooded floodplain in Plano, Illinois, through which Rock Creek runs; and my father and mother, Paul and Julia Holinger, who bought a cabin on a lake surrounded by forest north of Crivitz.

Acknowledgments

The author is truly grateful to the editors of the following magazines for publishing these poems, some gently revised:

Ailanthus: "Crivitz, Athelstane, Lena and Pound," "Acorns," "Sun Going Down on a Farm"

Another Chicago Magazine: "How I Spent My Vietnam," "Water Colors"

Boulevard: "Treasure"

Cider Press Review: "Abandoned, Gone"

The Country Mouse: "Naming the Galaxy"

Cumberlands: "Promised Weight"

Farmer's Market: "August Skies"

Format: "What the Poet Heard"

Ball State University Forum: "Late Arrivals, Early Beginnings," "Imagining What's Left," "Nesting Blue"

Hampden-Sydney Review: "Screaming Beneath the Ruins"

Interim: "Evolution"

International University Poetry Quarterly: "Monarchs"

Kansas Quarterly: "Its Coming"

Main Street Rag Bar Anthology: "All-You-Can-Eat Fish Fry"

Manhattan Poetry Review: "Counting Grapes," "Full Worm Moon"

NEBO: "Pearl and Ray's"

Newsletter Inago: "Communion," "What To Do in the Final Fifteen"

The Ohio Review: "Tired of Traveling"

Painted Bride Quarterly: "Moving Toward the Dance"

Red Cedar Review: "A Way Back In," "The World as Bowling Ball"

Two Hawks: "Up at the Cabin"

Wings Poetry Anthology: Bury Me Sioux: "When Oaks Have Pushed"

Contents

North of Crivitz

Travel north of Crivitz and redeem yourself.

Drive out past the Right-Turn-No-Stop,
wave to the firehouse dog,
accelerate at the dairy farm
whose fence shapes the world
for storybook cows
beside the paneless,
lopsided farmhouse circled
by red-brown prairie, beyond

which, needling north through woods—
dark and hallowed timbered caves—
you can let go, again become
someone you knew before the lust
for more of everything, when rising
each morning left you breathless,

the change as sure and final
as losing desire for desire.

Communion

I jog along a two-path lane
snaking under Norway pine,
conifer, birch, maple, and oak,
virgin forest untouched by fire.

Chicago is hours away.

There's one way to breathe
along Lake Michigan,
through Lincoln Park,
back down Lake Shore Drive.

There's another way to breathe
where air is redolent
of bark, sap, needles, and rot,
the woods' succulence
swilled, savored, swallowed,

the run so filling, I think,
This is where I could die.

Mechanics of Nature

A daddy longlegs whiskers
his way across the sill,
side-stepping pens and model boats,

his brown pea body buoyed
by thread-thin legs
bent for ups and downs

as if finding his way
over obstacles was reason
enough to feel.

Late Arrivals, Early Beginnings

Back in the cabin old friends loaned,
I stare at a wall of photographs
arranged like a large, uneven checkerboard.
I knew them when five, ten,
fifteen, twenty-years-old, but now
I hold them distant, as if my childhood
might turn on me
as growing older does.

Drawn to the center, I focus on twins
standing on the dock before swimming,
hair shiny and dry, figures afraid
of future cold, the high dive supports
rising behind them like conduits
from hidden springs.

In April, morning light arrives
by five, the conifers' black fur
silhouetted against a pigeon feather sky.
The lake still holds white snow,
only the fringe darkened by water
where orange needles fossilize
in shallow ice. Across the lake,
leafless brown maples tangle
with skeletal birches.

The weight of last night's silence
breaks with birds speaking
in foreign tongues. From this far
down the lake, the old high dive,
still standing, looks limber, sinewy,
waiting to spring.

Counting Grapes

The day it rained, we sat on the porch
pushing grapes with index fingers
into empty pockets of our mouths
until our jaws burned for relief.

As lips parted for a final insert,
the last became penultimate
as someone always fit another in,
like the time we drove to the Peshtigo

and beached on bald boulders
like sunning snakes. As the river thundered
below, you kissed me open-mouthed
and passed a grape saliva slick

I tasted and turned until you leaned
back and lifted your head
like ending a prayer,
and the fruit burst into flame.

Imagining What's Left

The night was too deep, and we were too tired
to clean the pike when we came in,
so we left it stringered to the dock
in one foot of water overnight.

Next morning we saw through white
pirouettes spinning over the ice-calm lake
only the head, mere fringes of meat
behind eyes, gills, and mouth, now resting
on the sand bottom littered
confetti white.

I wish I could have watched
the snapping turtle come upon
the chained fish, watch unbelieving eyes
gape at such a catch with steel steered
through gills, and having only back
and forth for escape.

Not wanting to go deeper, I unhook
the stringer from the post, and with metal clasps
ringing like wind chimes, hold the head
against the deepest blue the dawn sky holds,
and try to imagine what's becoming of me.

Crivitz, Athelstane, Lena, and Pound

Crivitz, Athelstane, Lena, and Pound,

names of towns thick in the vowels
and consonants of the Upper Midwest
where tractors hug hillsides
and dogs grill postmen
who fold IGA flyers
in lead boxes hanging
by one rusting screw
to the right of porch doors
behind which children grow out of

Crivitz, Athelstane, Lena, and Pound.

Promised Weight

Mother calls before I'm up to say
It was two years ago today he died.
I mumble words that help her,
But the reminder angers me,
For I no longer wish to grieve
By rote remembrance. But it's done,
And I think again of life, boxed
like a Marshal Field's gift,
Square and white, neatly tied,
As if he'd arranged it all:
The parties mother gave twice a year
For medical men from out of town
Catered on silver trays in which his name was cut.

One morning in June we fished the lake
Where steam curled over the surface
In slow ballet, lithe and white.
His hands, light as butterflies on the oars,
moved the boat with even strokes
as we cast toward shore where hidden deer
stomped and wheezed. We fished into the day,
catching crappie and pike we did not keep.
When something finally hit that promised
exciting weight, I leaned out, holding
the net to bring in whatever he had,
still out of sight, swimming scared,
searching for a fallen tree to wrap around
before pulled into the airy light of death.

Abandoned, Gone

The shed stood at the border of woods
surrounding the house. Who built it,
no one knew. Its sides and double doors
needed new paint. Inside, the scent
of history: mildew, decay, rubber,
and gasoline: Tires from vehicles
long vanished; chewed and tattered
canvas chairs; red metal gas
cans; wood-framed storms
spiderweb laced; keyless rider mower
& separate snowplow blade;
cardboard boxes stuffed with Frisbees,
balls and bats; brown corkboard
wall where silver stays stayed nothing.

Mice have the run of the place.
They scurry to safety when I open
the door, the outside light
blanketing interior junk I covet
still, God knows why. Maybe
because a graveyard resurrects
the dead—or at least the truly gone—
like inchoate ghosts haunting
the living into believing he wants
only the things he cannot explain.

Nearly Country

Down at the newsstand they unplugged
the humidor the day that Lotto came.

Mary, the pharmacist's daughter, sells scribbled-on middle
and high school texts half price from a box in the window seat.

What the barber hears first is "How's it been?"
"Gimme a trim," and "Little off around the ears."

The restaurant out on County X has framed
a *Bus Stop* Marilyn over the men's room sink.

Quacks and sharks build reputations stenciled
in golden caps on windows blinded by boredom.

The Neighborhood Nook sells everything it did when I
lived here, except the shelf of DVDs where hats once hung.

Mr. Cox, who lost an arm in France, has left
The Rugged Man to Paul, who lost a leg in Nam.

Two or three miles out of town a gray, windowless
house leans over, spent, beside a field of corn.

The creek whose once whitewater flooded pastures where cattle
grazed now's cough dry till we get spring melt or three-day rain.

There's talk of Amtrak fixing up the station stop, talk
heard before, but as for now the trains still whistle through.

Artists and Anglers

You can fish all night and still return empty.
Nothing has gone for lures cast to shallow
underwater brush or out to deep, dark cool.

So why persist, why wander back to ponds when day gives up
to night, the sun soon hidden by Norway, birch,
and tamarack, to throw in with plum-purple surface ripples,
silence so pure it deafens, lonely air harboring thoughts
of morning mist, and woods turned black as rain-soaked bark?

Because poets and anglers sit side by side in the boat,
equally at ease floating over paper or water, conforming
to conscience and imagined invisibles, never succumbing
to belittling the little, the less, the loner, the lost.

Not a calling. Rather a hymn hummed internally,
its rhythms urgent as those of the largemouth bass
spearing up through lily pads, setting his sights
on what there is at hand, whatever lures
him out of his depths.

A Way Back In

Withered leaves hang like shredded chamois
as dusk darkens snow to stone,
the creek to ink.

Rising over my way back in,
the moon is framed by two slate trees
and I, standing at the edge of woods,

am like some ancient mathematician
bedazzled to discover his Stonehenge,
by some outrageous miracle,

has worked.

Monarchs

In August we reap our older thoughts,
odd memories plated in afternoons of gold
like passions spent in scratchy haylofts,
naked weights, torn and full of folds.

By seven we can stare into the sun
as though the summer were to end tonight.
We wait as if to watch the season drop, undone,
its fields browning under new ivory light.

The greens of tired days when shade and birds
filled fuller trees are lost to boughs of turning oaks
whose leaves already spot the ground, withered,
wrinkled, undisturbed by moon that soaks

the eastern sky in orange round. And here,
to magnify the move to fall, still monarchs cleave
to branches, leaf on leaf, as if they would revere
this rest from flight, this momentary night's relief.

Box Elder Bugs

We can't believe it when one of our friends
takes out a dime and makes it vanish
from his hand, only to find it
behind an ear, and then inside a cup.

Someone suggests a walk. The forest floor,
crusted with snow, scratches tinted eyes.
Beside the dam my grandfather built
to keep his cattle downstream, my father
piled concrete blocks, "To fill where water
threatens curling back on itself."

When I say that water never takes to dams,
someone quotes Frost on fences and neighbors.

Back by the fire, I bathe in afternoon light
pouring in through windows, scorching
black box elder bugs crossing the panes,
silhouettes striped with orange veins
disappearing with the waning afternoon
like the magic of losing dimes.

Moving Toward the Dance

Morning's first breath of light whispers coals
alive behind the hill where Burlington
freights wheeze cargoes along their east-west run.
I think about committing myself to cold,
chapped floors scattered with chipped ceiling leaves, folds
in clothes, and missing buttons exposed, undone.
I look outside for deer; they have begun
to eat the bark off logs piled near the road.

My finding them brings dark remembrance;
they move from nibbling on fringes, their hides
dun as November dusk, their heights enhanced
by early dreams. When they begin to prance
over grasses like five Great Danes, I glide
with them, feeling like moving toward the dance.

Two Orioles Swim

Two orioles swim
    in the air above
        the June-thick bank
where weeping willows sway
    above curlicue currents
        and smallmouth bass swirl for food.

Downstream, a soft-shell turtle's
    ancient medieval shield fossils
        in bottomless bank mud
as a snapping turtle drags
    its shell from shore to river
        floor, lime-moss archipelago exposed.

A shiny cowbird flutter-dances
        beneath a peony blossom
            black ants lick into bloom.

As sun coats trash trees—
    hackberry, mulberry, cypress,
        linden, poplar, cottonwood, elm—
poison ivy vines slide anaconda
    length up tree trunks
        through prickly summer detritus.

Along a road no longer a road,
    pink bull thistles, columbine,
        dame's rocket, and big blue stem
grow where thirty years ago red
    Chevy pickups, blue station wagons,
        and black 4-wheelers flew by, now only a distant

rush, a mile or so over,
      moving to much the same place,
         everywhere but here.

Its Coming

When the heat woke him up,
her face was turned to the night,
her eyes the color of the moon,
and he did not say her name.
When the doctor came, he said,
"Just slipped naturally, best way
for anyone or anything." He thought,
"Then why did she twitch?"
and finally thought it best to ask.
"Muscles are the last to stop," the doctor said.
"Takes time for death to penetrate."

He thought this over every time he watched
a new night move in from the east.
She knew too much about survival
to be unfamiliar with its opposite;
she'd never gotten into anything
before she thought it proper for a woman
of her place and parentage. She'd get along
without him over there somehow,
just like he had managed here. And, certainly,
she'd have relations to visit with.

Tonight he must have lingered longer
than he thought. He couldn't see
if the door to the barn was shut.
Too late to wander out.
Nothing there to get out anymore anyhow;
he shut it only for appearances.
Time now for something warm,
to get to bed, to wait for its coming.

All-You-Can-Eat Fish Fry

By the time you set your boots
up top the barstool rung,
Bill's already drawing the Bud,
the glass delivered on a napkin
covered with cartoon jokes.
On the jukebox someone's quartered
Dolly Parton, big again now
her TV show and loss of weight
has everyone talking, and by the end
of the night, "Happy Birthday"
will hold everyone in a sing-along.
No crowd now, but wait till stores
get out, people coming for
the All-You-Can-Eat Fish Fry,
your choice of whitefish or cod,
every Friday night. Down along the bar
sit feed and tractor hats, but you like it
over by the window, listening to who
phones out, and after dinner Rosie the bag lady
comes by here and sits herself down
on the window ledge beside you.
And there's no better seat if there's a fire
or accident in town or out on Highway 34
for seeing trucks whine out the station
kitty-corner, not to mention from here
seeing every stool and table inside, even
a look behind the bar back to the kitchen
where the college dropout wears his FISHFEST
T-shirt and dangles a cigarette over the bin
of french fries and onion rings.

How I Spent My Vietnam

1

Early September. On back roads and interstates
black and orange caterpillars inch their way across,
all headed one way. Two vermillion drops
of last night's Port spread across the kitchen table.

2

Five years before, when there was time enough,
it seemed, for them to send us all, the fraternity
waited for the living room TV to pull birthdays
from a spinning bin. As soon as the drawing began,
and every few minutes afterward, a brother
would hold his head, then leave for any
of several bars. By the end of the lottery,
the college had moved downtown,
some to celebrate, others forgetting
that which they didn't already know.
Those of us who fell in the middle drank
in uncertainty, stared at the casualties,
and understood what we took for immortality
two hours ago was only a poor excuse for hope.

3

"And that's the way it is…" is how my Vietnam
ended each night. With greasy hands I threw the chicken
bones in supermarket bags two-ply thick.

4

I moisten a dishcloth to wipe off
last night's stains, leaving again the gray
surface smooth, unsticky, clear.
Outside, a monarch butterfly
circles a patch of zinnias. Good to know
at least one caterpillar's made it off
the roads unscathed—if ever
he even got near death.

Tired of Traveling

1

Before you leave the floodplain,
where not even seeds
of buds hint green in your eyes,
you leave the path for the creek

where the miracle you will remember
every time you see yellow
comes from a dead sapling

blossoming with hundreds of goldfinches
spilling their *chicory, chicory* song,
twitching nervous yellow wings
beneath black-capped crowns.

2

August. Dead heat on a day
that blisters life, even at dusk.
The sun grows large inside
green wombs of oaks.

Out for a walk, you follow
a tipsy monarch around low boughs
to where, weighing down a limb,
hundreds of monarch wings believe
they're maples, fluttering into flame.

Naming the Galaxy

In China they call the vast
ocean of stars a Silver River,
turning seacoasts to banks,
tides to currents,
islands to sandbars.

The spilled Milky Way
moniker pours
from Middle English,
derived from the Latin
"via lactea."

Gazing up,
body cocooned in quilts
on a dark Wisconsin dock,
the whip-poor-wills' song drowned
silent hours ago by night's deep dark,
only a lonely car or two whirring past
a mile away through woods on County C,
the white-speckled stillness,
transcending all else, is still, to me,
untranslatable.

Watercolors

My wife watercolors in the kitchen.
"I can't make the transition from lights
to darks where everything looks real.
it's scary to go on."

She goes back to it after lunch,
filling in the piled wood, the shack
that stores summer screens, the gravel
road, and over lawns the oak shadows
twist anaconda length.

"It's terrible and it's done, maybe," she says,
"because you can't go over water,
water dries." I say, "I don't see why
you'd want to go back over anything."

I hear the rush of water and cleaning
of porcelain, imagine rainbows
circling in the sink, wasted colors
dropping into pipes too wet
for anything to stick for long and think
I'll have to have it framed.

The Give and Take of Indoor Birdwatching

Seed, sock, and suet block
draw them here, store-bought
nature on display to serve them
better than flower, bark, or earth.

Binoculars bring them closer still,
through Thermo pane where we inspect
their every line and color matched
with photo-perfect Petersons
needed to differentiate Hairy
from Red-bellied, sparrow from wren,
nuthatch from chickadee. Birders

we're not, not those who wade death-
still deep in pre-dawn light
swamped in khaki and leather
focused on nature in the raw,
practiced in winged, crowned,
and breasted eyes scouring bough, bog,
grass, log, and water for colors crisp
as mid-ships' ensigns coming home
to roost, oracular spectacles feeding beak
to beak their future kind. We, here inside

our forced-air room, cannot compete
with outdoor drama, our birdsong muted
and glass obstructing natural scent.
And yet I'd rather nest alongside you
(in wooden chairs while breakfasting
on eggs and bacon), the only flight
my glance that's taking wing in yours.

Up at the Cabin

Up at the cabin, a rainbow trout learns to woo young women fishing from the bank.

Up at the cabin, thunderstorms flood our shoes if left on the steps.

Up at the cabin, an ornithologist wearing khaki pants and shirt grows eagle talons to shred a Wheaties box.

Up at the cabin, felines perch on the roofs to stare in skylights like Peeping Toms.

Up at the cabin, crystal shatters when awe-struck.

Up at the cabin, the closeted .22 shoots blanks at snapping turtles in its sleep.

Up at the cabin, golf carts belch candy and do wheelies when not spinning donuts.

Up at the cabin, children weigh down a raft's corner before age overtakes them.

Up at the cabin, cars drive to the dump to see miracles.

Up at the cabin, water balloons explode and leave a desert stain.

Up at the cabin, paddle a kayak and never again feel the need to vote.

Up at the cabin, fish feed over camouflaged humans hovering until nightfall.

Up at the cabin, ecstasy flits like a hummingbird foreshadowing blossom thrust.

Treasure

We helped our father dig the holes,
then hauled the burlap sacks
crammed with roots and dirt
halfway down the bank where level
interrupted fall for forty feet.
They took, and he expected fruit
in fall. Not until first snow
would he admit sterility.
He spent the winter drawing lines
of hose we helped dig trenches for
in spring. When elegant connections
concocted from spigot to hose
to hose to hose were closed,
the tap was turned, and sprinklers
sprang into blossom below.
but that wasn't it. Next year
we fertilized, then aerated,
and so on until he died.

Last time he left his bed
he tried to rip out baseboards
with a broken thistle stick
while muttering something about
the man who owned this place
before him must have died with money
hidden when banks went belly-up.
We searched each other speechlessly.
Sure, he was old and sick, but what
if he was right? Then common sense
helped grab the stick and pull him,
screaming, back to bed. He died
so silently a few weeks later
we ate Easter dinner undisturbed.

Cremation followed. I suggested
his remains be spread among
the apple trees. Erosion had by then
unearthed the labyrinth of hose
now hacked apart by mower or removed
for other jobs. The season's early
prairie cover stretched beneath
his leafless trees. I spread gray ashes
over pink spring beauties, then,
as others prayed in town his soul
ascend and enter heaven,
I fetched the crowbar from my car
and ran downstairs, itching to harvest
what dream, insanity, or treasure
he imagined left behind.

Evolution

Here no silent eye winks garage doors up.
I kill the engine, let songbirds filter
back through colander trees, let squirrels claw
to spiral heights, and then make for the bank
where in the creek below a heron lifts
on wings of blue-gray quilts.
The lazy carp with curled lips
and flash-bulb bellies continue
sucking along the muddy floor,
backs snaking up shallows
as if to gain dry land.

I cross the field to the dry October runoff creek
where leaves confetti rose, yellow, orange the earth,
where half-buried stones, rotten logs, and roots
like rusted prison bars bring me back to life.

When voices swim over invisible falls
I climb behind bushes that let me watch
without being seen. Two rifled boys wander below.
"The sign said back there said 'Wildlife Preserve.'
All I seen is deer tracks and a woodchuck hole."
"Animals can't read," the other says as he searches
for something to shoot while his friend unzips
to take a leak. "I wonder if anyone lives around here."
"Who cares?" replies the filler of dry creeks.

Their natural current carries them
twisting through woods, an uneven course
under shadows winter will whiten like ugly skin
across which varicose veins will slide
till spring returns water to land
and the heron will hang and fall flightless,
and the carp will turn back to the sea.

Pearl and Ray's

in chipped red, capitals
arced in a quarter moon tells
passers-by who waits and cooks.

Inside, behind
the torn green shades,
gray men click forks
on heavy plates
and women, two-handed,
lift green-lipped mugs.

They blow noses in napkins pulled
from Hav-A-Naps,
butter and syrup wheat cake stacks,
pour milk from silver creamers
into a Kellogg's box grabbed
from a lineup above mirrored pies
half-gone.

One straw hat waits
on a wooden rack.

Pearl clears away what's left,
changes cream,
pours water into plastic cups.
From in back, Ray calls,
"Short stack up, scramble'n ham,"
enough to know he's there
readying what she is to serve.

Full Worm Moon

March 25th. Tonight
the radio reports
a Full Worm Moon
when worms turn,
push upward, transcend
their lot, coming out
to breathe in lunar light.

Stirred from earth, they snake
over sidewalks, backyards,
and turned-over, clodded cornfields
lying under the white chalk night
passed through on a half-hour ride back
from teaching night class in DeKalb.

At home in the driveway
I listen with the windows down
for worms digging skyward.
I'm ready to follow
the first one I hear.

August Skies

Saturday, August 1: Lammas

The earth has come halfway to fall
from summer's stretch in June,
but here there is no Lammas feast,
no field, no corn, no first crop.

In place of fields
beyond this suburb beyond suburbs,
raw frames grow,
insulation silvering the 2 X 4s,
thermal panes and sliding doors
glassing treeless Midwest light.

Indoors, we harvest laundry,
feed on freezer bags,
reap naps in basement chairs.

Tonight we'll celebrate a wedding
at a local country club
that prides itself on natural air
guaranteed to soak men's suits,
paint the golf course blue,
and deliver to the newlyweds—
both divorced with kids—
a long, lean night
of cornucopic ripening.

Sunday, August 9: Full Moon

We've watched it build in evening skies
even as the sun supports
the softball leagues on crusty turf

and fishermen below the dam.
We stand at the end
of our dead-end street
by a cornfield left to fireflies
until next year when promises
have threatened going farther,
past new two-story townhomes
to the K-Mart/Jewel mall.

In June we watched jade pandemonium
rain up through stalks that shield
us from vapor lights fogging the parking lot.
This afternoon's storm has given earth
a river's smell of arrogance,
the Green Corn Moon behind us
blossoming beneath a cloud
as if by chance.

We're back from a party
for a nephew turning two;
both sides of the family came
and after greeting on a backyard slab,
we chose sides like a grammar school dance.
The boy tore through
his plastic toys and OshKosh jeans

until the parents brought out beer
and dip and whole-grain snacks.
The mother's mother undressed her tomato aspic
as an uncle on the father's side
reheated eggplant Parmesan.

By the time the boy found something worth his time—
a horn he honked the rest of the afternoon—
the older children took turns splitting chairs, trees,

and relatives with a plastic red and yellow chainsaw.
As my leg was cut off at the knee the fourth time in an hour,
I glimpsed the moon between belligerent clouds and wished
I was seeing it at the end of a dead-end street.

Monday, August 10: Sirius

The Dog Star gleams in pre-dawn east,
a sign for Egyptians the Nile will flood,
a sign to Greeks that summer's heat
will dry as dry as Dryden's *Aeneid:*
        "So Sirius, flashing forth in sinister lights,
            Pale human kind with famine frights."
"Bickering red and emerald" (according to Tennyson),
it slips away, inevitably, as morning's Monet shades
again the temperatures into record heat.

I wander into the TV room
where twenty-two TV movies wait.

Wednesday, August 12: Perseid Meteor Showers Begin

The northern constellation Perseus seems
a sender of meteors, silent, white-thread lines
connecting silver points on a black-paper sky.

At Mother's farm in Plano, Illinois,
I wait for a telephone "field technician";
being a weekend retreat, there's no one here
admitting repairs. As soon as his Chevy rumbles away,
I walk through prairie above the floodplain
and run-off creeks where I find the flower

often mistaken for Queen Anne's lace,
the Cow's Parsnip, lacking the purple star
at the heart of the Queen's brocade.

Drifting back toward the house
I wander across my brother's garden
where weeds have not yet quite consumed
the lot: pumpkins build to football size,
and lines of zinnias bob shiny
red and orange and pink and purple globes
above green-leaf confusion
underneath which, nearly hidden,
a low, white fence is meant
to keep out rabbits, woodchucks,
and cautionary deer.

A pale yellow Sulphur butterfly
feeds silently, its black-ringed wings
like parchment's ancient script.
Cicadas and grasshoppers swarm
in a shower of song,

the top of the prairie shudders
as invisible animals trundle away,
White Cabbage butterflies
glide to late clover,
and black-winged hornets
stroll pink bull thistle blossoms.

Above, a front moves in.

Monday, August 24: New Moon

The faculty meeting for the new year
begins with a prayer and ends with beer.

In between we're told to be enthusiasts,
encourage thought,
and watch for gum in class.
It's a new beginning,
our leader monotones,
A time to try new methods
within, of course,
the traditional framework.

By the time I get out
it's past 9:30 and dark. Driving home
past dwindling cornfields—
and subdivisions sprung up overnight—
I see the moon's sliver of light
at the edge of its hideous shadow,
its silver ascent aimed at the bleak
desolation including us all,
even when doing 45 in a 30,
even if dreaming of August skies
that now seem light years away
that I have faith will ripen again
in spite of these thoughts of never.

Acorns

The stone millhouse half a mile south
is now City Hall, and here the posts
that held the iron wheel that raised
and lowered the iron plate, which raised
and lowered the mill race
that regulated the grind, have rotted out,
allowing everything once dammed
at will now through.

Across the water a shotgun's shout
filters through woods that think of giving up
their green for sunset colors. Take

the man here this morning, before
the hunter, while deer were on the move.
Acorns pelted him like after heavy rains
when wind comes back to dry the trees. He covered
his head and watched the acorns roll
down the wide dirt path. On top of the bank
eroded in a sideways U where creek
breaks back toward river, he saw the water
changed from glass to mud with downpours
flooding county roads in northeast Illinois.

The creek was high, not enough to challenge
shape, but high enough to alter islands:
the gravel isthmus near his shore was gone;
limbs and water grass broke the far
bank's surface. He remembered reading
Freud on dreams: that only there
there is no "No," where the hare will shoot
the sportsman dead if given the shells
and half a chance.

But now there's no one here to hear the shotgun blast,
fired perhaps by a zealous rabbit, intent
on downing the hunter come out of his hole
to take advantage of fall before winter freezes
everything still. The acorns by then, buried
in earth, are dreaming of nights when spring's warm pull
will trigger their chance to explode into light.

Screaming Beneath the Ruins

My friend brings in his poetry to resurrect
My classes buried in American lit
Before the Twains and Hemingways.
Next day, a boy with brass proposes that
The poet's perverted because at sixty
He writes about a boy who follows
Three co-eds into the GIRLS bathroom.

I tell him that's what poetry is, wish
Fulfillment, steam released from one's
Unconscious mind. He says he's never been
Unconscious, and if he has any say about
Our reading list from here on in,
He'll never read verse again.

This morning at breakfast I asked my wife
How the New Horizons Oat Bran Cereal,
That would lower cholesterol, fiber a colon,
And cover the vitamin alphabet, tastes.
"Coarser than sand and harder than rock," she says.
"Why do we kill ourselves to survive?" I add,
pouring a heaping bowl of Cap'n Crunch.

Tonight I watch Armenian cranes pinch concrete slabs
From concrete mounds like truck stop quarter games
Picking out plastic globes with 5-cent rings.
Three days ago the earth shook at 11:41 a.m.,
A time of safety in schools, stores, and businesses.
The deaths, an expert says, are not from crush
Of wall alone, but the breathing in of leftover dust.
By telephone a man reports in broken English
There's still screaming beneath the ruins,
Showing there's life below.

The World as Bowling Ball

Heard in the class before mine,
Physics or Theology, that if the world
were compressed into a one-foot sphere
it would be smooth as a bowling ball.

Driving home that afternoon I see
forests splintered into water,
mountains chipped to sand,
cities atomized, jungles dusted,
the earth's core collapsed.

It isn't easy driving through such terrain
where everything is more confused than waking
from a mid-day nap to the ringing of a phone.

I steer for the edge, hoping somehow
to stick to the world's slippery skin.

What the Poet Heard

As an alternative in the Arts,
the government suggests sending poets
back to caves. There, in the cool, wet-drip darkness
they chisel into stone sounds
that will not yellow for fifty million years.

Though wind and water massage the edge
of message, the cold divisions still seem apart
from lichened chaos spread over the rest of rock.

And if the archeologist will listen,
he may hear what the poet heard,
breaking bits of stone on stone,
and may hear the poet, petrified
he will not survive, howling
from the deepest, blackest corner of his cave.

Grubs

Come May, the grackles settle onto lawns
to listen for the shift of grubs whose lack
of light will never know the break of dawns
for rooting food. Their microbe meals taken black,
consumed in pallid ecstasy, when
tweezer beaks break earth's osmotic feed
for indigent dissolve beyond dirt's pen
in midnight fowl's guts forever freed.

If pulling for the stronger being chafes
your sentimental whim, consider please
that you and I, who live as if we're safe
from prey who graze and kill with ease,
are never so much like those underground
when cancer, stroke, or heart attack reach down.

When Oaks Have Pushed

"There's a saying," an old woman says,
"Put in corn when oaks have pushed their leaves
far as a mouse's ears; what Ceres
told Triptolemus before Sicily."

Sitting beside a field on dry, cracked stumps,
three aging farmers and one of their sons
speak to each other with familial pomp
of spring's last frost laid out like fanon.

Broken sod crests on waves beneath dipping
swallows in shoreless, rusty flight, seas plowed
to depths that summon ichthys nibbling
up to rowed seed last year left fallowed.

It is only now that the son will hold
all things apart. He listens to differences,
his ear catching time in a church bell,
the planting set by older, seasoned senses.

Later he will sit and talk around fields
that do not tell its soil from the water,
that praise any god for bringing yields
out of darkness into blue swallowed air.

Sun Going Down on a Farm

Then he left her
leaning against the porch railing
where the bare, gray wood
had worked off most of the paint.
She watched as the Riviera with its V-8
she'd gone with him to buy
rattled away through as much smoke
as it was making noise.

Her eyes grazed
to the top of the tree line
beyond the last field of corn.
When the sun was low enough
to see into, sometimes
a cloud of birds
would silhouette the sunset.

But tonight there are only the poplar and oak
patiently waiting to bury the failing, thickening light.
She sits on the swing and listens to rusted chains
squeaking monotonously over cicadas' screams.
As woods grip fast the rounded fire in branched black web,
she drifts across the porch on a Midwestern sea,
lifted on orange swells into the burning house,
knowing the trees will never again have the strength to hold.

Nesting Blue

We walk along the ridge of the ravine
where we're thinking of adding a porch.
The flaking paint is studded
with black box elder bugs.
"Bees don't build on anything blue,"
my sister says. "They think it's the sky."

As we round the edge of the house
my nephew Chris is standing by the pool
drained for winter.
He shouts: "A snake in here!"
A garter snake waves its tongue
and cocks its head above a rusted leaf,
its tapered tail suspended question-marked
above the dark, fall-buried floor.
"He wants to get out," Chris says.

Inside the house, death's cleaning clears the shelves of relics
from when my father lived there. "Anyone want a St. Francis?"
my wife throws out as she puts the wooden priest in a box
we'll send to Mother. "Can everyone live without ceramic birds?"
Down come the cardinal, the robin, the blue jay, the goldfinch.

I sit on a stone that keeps cars off the lawn.
In my journal I write, *Chris and I cut down*
three dead trees and sawed them into firewood.
The farmer who lives up the road dries harvested corn,
his tractor's thunder tumbling over our acres
of natural prairie evenly brown as sky.
Behind the softball field, a row of maples,
the only form imposed on nature by a grandfather
I never met, burns like setting suns.

Chris comes to the door, climbs down the steps, and runs
to where he found the snake. He believes he's alone.
"God," he gasps, "there's two of them—no, three!"
Whatever snakes possess holds him to the edge
as bees circle from a distance, avoiding
his shirt's limitless blue, finally leaving
for darker, less infinite shades.

What to Do in the Final Fifteen

Over the only station still on,
the word is delivered:
the bombs are on the way.
You have a quarter hour
to take cans and water
to the basement as if a tornado
would come. Scurry,
you're cornered.

The Existentialists once said
there was only one question to ask:
To suicide or not? Now
the question is: What to do
in the final fifteen-minute skit?

Here is one suggestion: Lean
a ladder up to the first branch
of the oldest tree
covering the house
like a comfortable cloud.
Follow lifting limbs
far as you can go. Carry
there your father's binoculars
he used for watching birds.

Hold on to the wood.
Listen to songbirds' trills.
Talk of life on the wing.

Al Warner: A Wildlife Narrative Fantasy

Before first light Al slides into tan
chamois shirt, trousers cut
from deerhide downed with arrows
feathered from shotgunned drakes,
calf-high boots snake- and waterproof,
twelve-inch knife sheathed on three-inch belt
patched together with skins of water rats.

He leaves the cabin for woods—
jack pine, blue spruce, water birch, oak—
footfalls silenced by rust-needled floor.
Looking skyward, the snake skinner
slithers through paths between overhead foliage,
the heavens, not earth, his guide.

Climbing handsawn boughs nailed to gnarled bark,
Al perches above what haunts below,
body and mind waiting berry still,
ant-bite bird-drop bee-sting immune,
the hunker down in morning's burnt dawn.

When shadows dapple apple-red maples,
black-blemished beeches, and *fleur-de-lis* ferns,
the buck moves in, less seen and heard
than felt and stirred till visible fills
invisible like a miracle,
hoof-steady stag with eye-steady gaze
tearing low roughage off undergrowth,
lost to what is already settled above.

Al draws bow's pulleyed pounds slowly
as gaining weight, Cyclops sight fixing
shaft's steel blades on helpless pulse.
Loosest when tension is greatest, Zen-lost
in string, limb, arrow, earth, firmament, cosmos,
Al whispers release, as sure of the kill
as lips pressed to an ear breathe love.

Afterward, he Bowies clean the carcass, bathes
in thick, warm blood, cuts his weight
in meat, leaves the rest for foragers;
even Al can only carry out so much beneath
braided branches, now luminous with light ever so holy.

Bluebells in the Time of Coronavirus

We cut a path through bluebells powdering
The woods, and as you bent to put a hand
Down to a white variety, you called to me,
Stopped on the wooden bridge
Whose guardrail had rotted and fallen
Into the runoff creek full with last night's rain.

You looked as if the flower caught
You by surprise and changed
The way you lived. When finally
Crossing the path that took us back,
Farther up that mowed and trampled earth,
You called again, this time looking up from

A barn red trillium at what you thought
A heron, I an eagle, my vision no less
Or more than yours because it isn't
Names or who identifies what flies
Beyond our knowing that make one
Any more safe or fortunate. Once wings

Were lost beyond the reach of branches shamrock
Starred, we moseyed on, grounded in banter
About our son and daughter, living now
In the spring of their age, to us
Uniquely hued, like that rare afternoon
Through which we strolled toward home.

About the Author

Richard Holinger's poetry, fiction, creative nonfiction, and book reviews have appeared in *The Southern Review, The Iowa Review, Boulevard, Witness,* and been nominated for three Pushcart Prizes. His collection, *Not Everybody's Nice,* won the 2012 Split Oak Press Flash Prose Chapbook Contest. An innovative fiction chapbook, *Hybrid Seeds: Little Fictions,* was published by Kattywampus Press. A collection of his newspaper columns, *Kangaroo Rabbits and Galvanized Fences,* by Dreaming Big Press, 2020. Recently retired after forty years at Marmion Academy (Aurora IL), he currently facilitates a writing workshop and lives with his wife, dog, and occasionally his two adult children in the Fox River Valley, an hour west of Chicago. Degrees include a Ph.D. in Creative Writing from The University of Illinois at Chicago, and an M.A. in English from Washington University (St. Louis). Before teaching full time, he worked as a busboy, stock boy, groundskeeper, and security guard.

You can find more about Richard Holinger's poetry at:

richardholinger.net

www.ingramcontent.com/pod-product-compliance
Lightning Source LLC
Chambersburg PA
CBHW031152090426
42738CB00008B/1298